Francis Frith's
Monmouthshire

Photographic Memories

Francis Frith's
Monmouthshire

Tony Cornish and James Plant

FRITH
BOOK Co

First published in the United Kingdom in 2002 by
Frith Book Company Ltd

Hardback Edition 2002
ISBN 1-85937-532-4

British Library Cataloguing in Publication Data

Francis Frith's Monmouthshire
Tony Cornish and James Plant

Frith Book Company Ltd
Frith's Barn, Teffont,
Salisbury, Wiltshire SP3 5QP
Tel: +44 (0) 1722 716 376
Email: info@francisfrith.co.uk
www.francisfrith.co.uk

Printed and bound in Great Britain

Front Cover: Abergavenny, Cross Street 1893 32596

AS WITH ANY HISTORICAL DATABASE THE FRITH ARCHIVE IS CONSTANTLY BEING CORRECTED AND IMPROVED
AND THE PUBLISHERS WOULD WELCOME INFORMATION ON OMISSIONS OR INACCURACIES

Contents

Francis Frith: *Victorian Pioneer*

FRANCIS FRITH, Victorian founder of the world-famous photographic archive, was a complex and multi-talented man. A devout Quaker and a highly successful Victorian businessman, he was both philosophic by nature and pioneering in outlook.

By 1855 Francis Frith had already established a wholesale grocery business in Liverpool, and sold it for the astonishing sum of £200,000, which is the equivalent today of over £15,000,000. Now a multi-millionaire, he was able to indulge his passion for travel. As a child he had pored over travel books written by early explorers, and his fancy and imagination had been stirred by family holidays to the sublime mountain regions of Wales and Scotland. 'What a land of spirit-stirring and enriching scenes and places!' he had written. He was to return to these scenes of grandeur in later years to 'recapture the thousands of vivid and tender memories', but with a different purpose. Now in his thirties, and captivated by the new science of photography, Frith set out on a series of pioneering journeys to the Nile regions that occupied him from 1856 until 1860.

Intrigue and Adventure

He took with him on his travels a specially-designed wicker carriage that acted as both dark-room and sleeping chamber. These far-flung journeys were packed with intrigue and adventure. In his life story, written when he was sixty-three, Frith tells of being held captive by bandits, and of fighting 'an awful midnight battle to the very point of surrender with a deadly pack of hungry, wild dogs'. Sporting flowing Arab costume, Frith arrived at Akaba by camel seventy years before Lawrence, where he encountered 'desert princes and rival sheikhs, blazing with jewel-hilted swords'.

During these extraordinary adventures he was assiduously exploring the desert regions bordering the Nile and patiently recording the antiquities and peoples with his camera. He was the first photographer to venture beyond the sixth cataract. Africa was still the mysterious 'Dark Continent', and Stanley and Livingstone's historic meeting was a decade into the future. The conditions for picture taking confound belief. He laboured for hours in his wicker dark-room in the sweltering heat of the desert, while the volatile chemicals fizzed dangerously in their trays. Often he was forced to work in remote tombs and caves where conditions were cooler. Back in London he exhibited his photographs and was 'rapturously cheered' by members of the Royal Society. His reputation as a photographer was made overnight. An eminent modern historian has likened their impact on the population of the time to that on our own generation of the first photographs taken on the surface of the moon.

Venture of a Life-Time

Characteristically, Frith quickly spotted the opportunity to create a new business as a specialist publisher of photographs. He lived in an era of immense and sometimes violent change. For the poor in the early part of Victoria's reign work was a drudge and the hours long, and people had precious little free time to enjoy themselves. Most had no transport other than a cart or gig at their disposal, and had not travelled far beyond the boundaries of their own town or village. However,

by the 1870s, the railways had threaded their way across the country, and Bank Holidays and half-day Saturdays had been made obligatory by Act of Parliament. All of a sudden the ordinary working man and his family were able to enjoy days out and see a little more of the world.

With characteristic business acumen, Francis Frith foresaw that these new tourists would enjoy having souvenirs to commemorate their days out. In 1860 he married Mary Ann Rosling and set out with the intention of photographing every city, town and village in Britain. For the next thirty years he travelled the country by train and by pony and trap, producing fine photographs of seaside resorts and beauty spots that were keenly bought by millions of Victorians. These prints were painstakingly pasted into family albums and pored over during the dark nights of winter, rekindling precious memories of summer excursions.

The Rise of Frith & Co

Frith's studio was soon supplying retail shops all over the country. To meet the demand he gathered about him a small team of photographers, and published the work of independent artist-photographers of the calibre of Roger Fenton and Francis Bedford. In order to gain some understanding of the scale of Frith's business one only has to look at the catalogue issued by Frith & Co in 1886: it runs to some 670 pages, listing not only many thousands of views of the British Isles but also many photographs of most European countries, and China, Japan, the USA and Canada – note the sample page shown above from the hand-written *Frith & Co* ledgers detailing pictures taken. By 1890 Frith had created the greatest specialist photographic publishing company in the world,

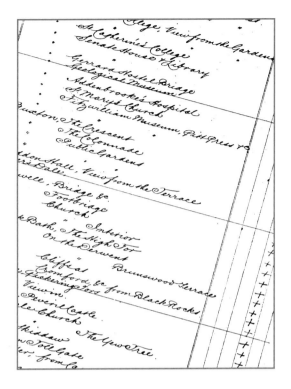

Frith's death, a new card measuring 5.5 x 3.5 inches became the standard format, but it was not until 1902 that the divided back came into being, with address and message on one face and a full-size illustration on the other. *Frith & Co* were in the vanguard of postcard development, and Frith's sons Eustace and Cyril continued their father's monumental task, expanding the number of views offered to the public and recording more and more places in Britain, as the coasts and countryside were opened up to mass travel.

Francis Frith died in 1898 at his villa in Cannes, his great project still growing. The archive he created continued in business for another seventy years. By 1970 it contained over a third of a million pictures of 7,000 cities, towns and villages. The massive photographic record Frith has left to us stands as a living monument to a special and very remarkable man.

with over 2,000 outlets – more than the combined number that Boots and WH Smith have today! The picture on the right shows the *Frith & Co* display board at Ingleton in the Yorkshire Dales. Beautifully constructed with mahogany frame and gilt inserts, it could display up to a dozen local scenes.

Postcard Bonanza

The ever-popular holiday postcard we know today took many years to develop. In 1870 the Post Office issued the first plain cards, with a pre-printed stamp on one face. In 1894 they allowed other publishers' cards to be sent through the mail with an attached adhesive halfpenny stamp. Demand grew rapidly, and in 1895 a new size of postcard was permitted called the court card, but there was little room for illustration. In 1899, a year after

Frith's Archive: *A Unique Legacy*

FRANCIS FRITH'S legacy to us today is of immense significance and value, for the magnificent archive of evocative photographs he created provides a unique record of change in 7,000 cities, towns and villages throughout Britain over a century and more. Frith and his fellow studio photographers revisited locations many times down the years to update their views, compiling for us an enthralling and colourful pageant of British life and character.

We tend to think of Frith's sepia views of Britain as nostalgic, for most of us use them to conjure up memories of places in our own lives with which we have family associations. It often makes us forget that to Francis Frith they were records of daily life as it was actually being lived in the cities, towns and villages of his day. The Victorian age was one of great and often bewildering change for ordinary people, and though the pictures evoke an impression of slower times, life was as busy and hectic as it is today.

We are fortunate that Frith was a photographer of the people, dedicated to recording the minutiae of everyday life. For it is this sheer wealth of visual data, the painstaking chronicle of changes in dress, transport, street layouts, buildings, housing, engineering and landscape that captivates us so much today. His remarkable images offer us a powerful link with the past and with the lives of our ancestors.

Today's Technology

Computers have now made it possible for Frith's many thousands of images to be accessed almost instantly. In the Frith archive today, each photograph is carefully 'digitised' then stored on a CD Rom. Frith archivists can locate a single photograph amongst thousands within seconds. Views can be catalogued and sorted under a variety of categories of place and content to the immediate benefit of researchers.

Inexpensive reference prints can be created for them at the touch of a mouse button, and a wide range of books and other printed materials assembled and published for a wider, more general readership - in the next twelve months over a hundred Frith local history titles will be published! The day-to-day workings of the archive are very different from how they were in Francis Frith's time: imagine the herculean task of sorting through eleven tons of glass negatives as Frith had to do to locate a particular sequence of pictures! Yet

See Frith at www.francisfrith.co.uk

the archive still prides itself on maintaining the same high standards of excellence laid down by Francis Frith, including the painstaking cataloguing and indexing of every view.

It is curious to reflect on how the internet now allows researchers in America and elsewhere greater instant access to the archive than Frith himself ever enjoyed. Many thousands of individual views can be called up on screen within seconds on one of the Frith internet sites, enabling people living continents away to revisit the streets of their ancestral home town, or view places in Britain where they have enjoyed holidays. Many overseas researchers welcome the chance to view special theme selections, such as transport, sports, costume and ancient monuments.

We are certain that Francis Frith would have heartily approved of these modern developments in imaging techniques, for he himself was always working at the very limits of Victorian photographic technology.

The Value of the Archive Today

Because of the benefits brought by the computer, Frith's images are increasingly studied by social historians, by researchers into genealogy and ancestory, by architects, town planners, and by teachers and schoolchildren involved in local history projects.

In addition, the archive offers every one of us an opportunity to examine the places where we and our families have lived and worked down the years. Highly successful in Frith's own era, the archive is now, a century and more on, entering a new phase of popularity.

The Past in Tune with the Future

Historians consider the Francis Frith Collection to be of prime national importance. It is the only archive of its kind remaining in private ownership and has been valued at a million pounds. However, this figure is now rapidly increasing as digital technology enables more and more people around the world to enjoy its benefits.

Francis Frith's archive is now housed in an historic timber barn in the beautiful village of Teffont in Wiltshire. Its founder would not recognize the archive office as it is today. In place of the many thousands of dusty boxes containing glass plate negatives and an all-pervading odour of photographic chemicals, there are now ranks of computer screens. He would be amazed to watch his images travelling round the world at unimaginable speeds through network and internet lines.

The archive's future is both bright and exciting. Francis Frith, with his unshakeable belief in making photographs available to the greatest number of people, would undoubtedly approve of what is being done today with his lifetime's work. His photographs, depicting our shared past, are now bringing pleasure and enlightenment to millions around the world a century and more after his death.

Monmouthshire - *An Introduction*

MONMOUTHSHIRE IS A county of outstanding beauty, from the remote stillness of Llanthony Abbey to the bustle of the market town of Abergavenny, the majestic castles of Raglan and Chepstow and the haunting Tintern ruins; from the rolling hills to the healing scars of the former industrial areas, Monmouthshire encompasses the rich heritage and culture of Wales. Monmouthshire, like the other counties of Wales, has undergone several boundary changes: places such as Newport, which has recently been awarded city status, and the ancient fortress at Caerleon, home of one of the biggest and most important civil settlements of Roman Britain, have been taken out of its authority. However, despite all the changes Monmouthshire retains a rich history, which is captured to some extent in the pages of this book. We hope that you enjoy your journey through the county as much as we enjoyed our journey in the writing of it.

Abergavenny

Abergavenny, the first stop on our tour around the county of Monmouthshire, owes its foundation to the Roman conquerors and its development to the Norman ones. Its strategic position at the confluence of both the Usk and Monnow rivers is an obvious incentive for its establishment both as a stronghold and as a centre of trade. The first Roman settlement centred on the fort of Gobannium, sited here to safeguard the road to Usk. The arrival of the Normans, after the Conquest, began a new phase in the town's development. Hameline de Balun built a stronghold here, but this castle fell into the hands of the notorious William de Braose - he chose to celebrate the Christmas of 1176 in a rather novel, if bloody, way. In revenge for the killing of his uncle by the Welsh of Gwent, he disguised his intentions under the guise of a conciliatory and seasonal invitation to them to join him in the castle for the festivities. Once there, they were murdered.

By the medieval period, the town had a flourishing market occupying a site at the north end of the settlement; development of trade within the walls was taking place as well, as plots of land were divided up between various merchants. The town also continued to provide a place of protection for the surrounding population - whenever they found themselves under attack, they would herd themselves and their cattle and sheep through the Westgate and into safety.

Owain Glyndwr visited the town in 1404 and sacked it; this harsh treatment was once again meted out to the town during the Civil War in 1646, this time at the hands of the Parliamentarian forces under Fairfax. The town also elected to support the losing side in 1688 when it declared its support for James II over William III (the eventual victor). Punishment was not so harsh this time, and the town only suffered the financial loss of having its charter, first granted in 1639, suspended.

The markets continued to grow to the point that the 17th-century market hall, which by then blocked a large section of the street, would have to be rebuilt. John Nash, a Carmarthenshire architect who later achieved great fame and success and designed such buildings as the Haymarket Theatre and the Brighton Pavilion, built a replacement hall, but even that was soon too small. The present building was built in 1870, and today still holds a lively market several times a week, as well as being home to some of the council offices and a theatre. The traditional animal markets still attract many people from the region, who gather to sell their cattle and sheep in the traditional way. The livestock market is now confined to one particular area, but there was a time in the 19th century when it was possible to see someone selling their animals in the side-streets of the town.

One of the most outstanding buildings in Abergavenny is St Mary's priory church. Founded in 1087 as a Benedictine priory, it holds one of the finest collection of medieval monuments in Wales, and has been described as Wales's Westminster Abbey.

Abergavenny, The Deri from Bailey Park c1960 A9086
The Deri is one of the seven peaks surrounding the picturesque town of Abergavenny. The scene today is much the same as the one we see here. Note the rugby posts, ever a central theme in South Walian life, towards the left of the picture. The pitch shown here is now home to Abergavenny Rugby Club.

Abergavenny, The Castle 1893 32599
A stronghold of the de Braose family, the castle was briefly captured by the Welsh warlord Sytsylt ap Dyferwald. It was retaken by William de Braose; then, in order to demonstrate his supposed magnanimity to his former enemies, he invited Sytsylt, his son Godfrey and some of their retainers to Abergavenny to celebrate Christmas - where they were butchered one and all! The Welsh exacted their revenge when they captured the castle once more and burnt it. The ivy-clad walls pictured here are now cleared of ivy, and the walkways no longer exist. The castle now houses the town and district museum.

Abergavenny
Cross Street 1914 67667
This photograph is taken from the middle of the street looking up
towards the High Street. The shop midway up the street on the
right, on the corner of Monk Street, is no longer 'Saunders Reliable
Seeds' - it is now the Optic Shop - and has also been transformed
into a flat-roofed building, sad to say. The frontage on the far left
has been removed. Notice the car moving up the street away from
the camera and the dog crossing the street in the foreground
paying no attention to the camera whatsoever.

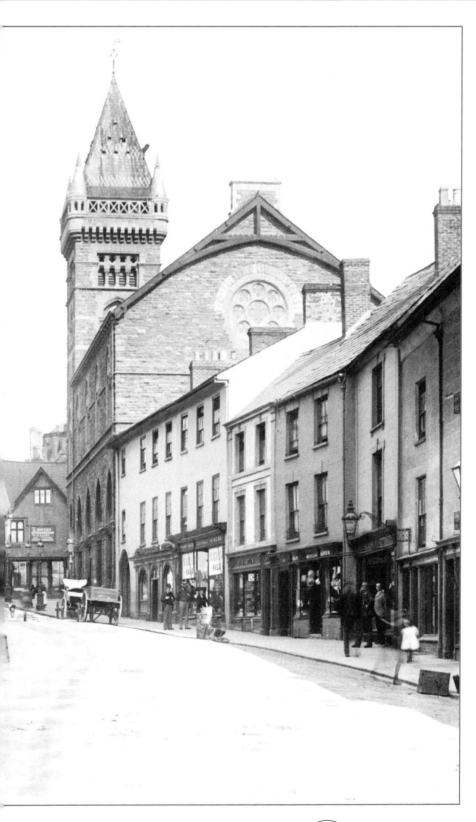

**Abergavenny
Cross Street 1893**
32596
The spire in the centre
of the picture stands
over the Town Hall and
Market Hall, with the
King's Head public
house just beyond. The
Angel Hotel on the left
is still in business, but
the post office on the
right has since been
relocated. Note the
crates placed
haphazardly on the left,
the two boys intently
watching the camera
and the ladders leaning
against the wall on the
left.

▼ **Abergavenny, St Mary's Church, the Interior 1898** 41678
This church was formerly the chapel of a small Benedictine priory founded by
Hameline de Balun. Nothing of this remains today - the present structure is mainly
14th-century. The window at the far end is now stained glass. The altar in this picture
has been moved slightly to the right, the chairs on the left have since been replaced
by pews, and the gaslights in the picture have been replaced by electric lighting.

▼ **Abergavenny, St Mary's Church, the Herbert Chapel 1898** 41680
This chapel houses the tombs of various members of the Herbert, Cantelupe and
Hastings families. The tomb of William ap Thomas (who died in 1446), father of the
first Earl of Pembroke, is in the centre. The chapel has recently been renovated.

▲ **Abergavenny
From the Canal 1893**
32587
A panoramic view of the
area, with Abergavenny in
the somewhat hazy
distance. Note the railway
sweeping round towards
the church in the centre
of the picture.

◀ **Abergavenny
The Sugarloaf from
Skirrid 1898** 41670
The town is overlooked by
the Sugarloaf and the two
Skirrids: Skirrid Fawr (large)
and Skirrid Fach (small).
Skirrid Fawr is both a place
of legend and of religious
significance - the cliffs on its
west side are said to have
resulted from an earthquake
at the time of the Crucifixion
of Jesus. It is still a place of
pilgrimage today.

◀ **Abergavenny
Holy Mountain 1898**
41674
Holy Mountain, otherwise known as Skirrid Fawr, is one of the seven hills surrounding Abergavenny. Standing at 1,595ft, the summit offers extensive views across the county.

◄ **Abergavenny
The Sugarloaf from
the River 1898** 41668
The house in the centre
of the picture is Nevill
Hall, which now forms
part of Nevill Hall
Hospital; it is also used
as a conference centre.

▼ **Abergavenny
The River Usk c1960**
A9035
Another general view,
this time of the tranquil
Usk as it wends its way
down towards the Severn
estuary south of
Newport, Gwent. The
Usk rises south-west
of Trecastle in Powys.

◄ **Abergavenny
Usk Bridge 1893** 32595
Just beyond this bridge
on the Monmouth road
we can seen the iron
railway bridge, which has
since been removed.
This view is very
different when rain falls
heavily upstream,
transforming this
peaceful view into a
raging torrent.

Abergavenny, Llanwenarth Church 1898 41683
This photograph shows the tranquil setting of St Peter's parish church, with its squat, crenellated tower and ivy-clad walls. The grass is cut rather shorter today.

Abergavenny, Llanwenarth Church, the Interior 1898 41684
The apparent plainness of the church interior is spectacularly offset by the stained glass window above the altar. Note the orders of service and hymn books out ready for the service.

Caldicot

Caldicot is famous for its Norman castle, which over the centuries has been adapted to suit the various conflicts in which it has played a part. The keep and curtain wall are thought to have been built around 1220 by Humphrey de Bohun, and the gatehouse was added in about 1381 by Thomas Woodstock, the third son of King Edward III. It was further developed in the Victorian period into a grand family house with some magnificent parkland, which can still be visited by the public.

Caldicot, The Village c1955 C544008

Although dominated by the castle, Caldicot's history goes back to Neolithic times, with constant occupation of the area throughout the Bronze and Iron Ages, the Roman period and of course medieval times. The Black Death decimated the population in 1349 and again in 1361, and the area suffered again in 1606 - this time many lives were lost in a severe flood. Despite these set-backs, the population slowly grew: in 1801 there were 465 inhabitants, in 1901 there were 1,196, and by 1951 the population had reached 1,770.

However, it was from this date that the real growth began. By 1961 the head count had almost doubled to 3,351, and by 1981 there were 9,394 inhabitants. This view of the village shows the Cross Inn in the centre of the picture - it is still in business. The pub on the right, the White Hart, has since been demolished; now Mr Chaplin's Taverna stands nearby.

Caldicot
The College c1965 C544023
Today, the college is part of a much bigger educational complex.
The town's growth was due to the arrival of industry and better
communications to the area. Llanwern Steelworks opened in 1962,
the Severn Bridge opened in 1966 and the M4 and the second
Severn crossing brought continued prosperity to the town. The
number of modern buildings in the town centre reflect this 20th-
century growth - but the castle still stands to remind us of
Caldicot's rich historic past.

Chepstow

This ancient walled town on the west bank of the River Wye is well-known for its castle perched high above the river. The town's Saxon name simply means 'market town', but to the Welsh it was known as 'Cas-Gwent'. Within ten years of the Battle of Hastings, William FitzOsbern had established a stone-built castle here, apparently not adhering to the established pattern of timber and earthwork motte and bailey first, followed by stone-built keep. This means that Chepstow is perhaps the earliest stone-built Norman castle in Wales. In 1072 a priory was also established here, and the town developed both as a market and as a centre of shipbuilding activities.

Backing the wrong side in a rebellion put paid to the aspirations of FitzOsbern's son, and in 1115 the Marcher lordship of Chepstow was granted to the de Clare family. Over the succeeding five generations the castle and the town went from strength to strength. In the 13th century it fell into the possession of the Bigods, also dukes of Norfolk, and then it passed to William Herbert, Earl of Pembroke, in the 15th century. Staunchly Royalist, Chepstow was besieged twice during the Civil War. It fell in 1645 after the starving garrison and its commander, Sir Nicholas Kemeys, fought to the death. The lower ward of the castle displays a memorial plaque to this feat of arms.

In the late 13th century a wall, known as the Portwall, was built on the landward side of the town; a town gate was also built, intended not as much for the defence of the town as for the control of goods going in and out. The town gate was rebuilt in the medieval period and again 'modernised' during the 16th century - the remnants can be seen today. The room above the town gate has had many uses over the years, including a prison, a guardroom and a home for the local constable. It has also housed the museum, although this is now located in a fine 18th-century townhouse near the castle.

Although it is steeped in history, Chepstow is perhaps best known for its racecourse set in 400 acres of beautiful parkland, which holds both flat and jump racing throughout the year.

**Chepstow
Disembarking from
Beachley Ferry 1950**
C77099
The Beachley Ferry
Hotel in this picture has
now changed its name
to the Old Ferry Inn;
the other buildings have
since been removed.
The slipway is still in
existence, but it is
primarily used for water
skiing - the existence of
the road bridge has
obviously killed off the
ferry trade from this
spot. This whole scene
is now completely
overshadowed by the
second Severn crossing
bridge. Note also the
motorcyclist with his
leather helmet on the
left of the picture.

**Chepstow
The 'Severn King'
Ferry Boat at
Beachley c1950**
C77097
There were three
ferryboats operating
here: the 'Severn
Queen', the 'Severn
Princess' and this one,
the 'Severn King'. Both
the 'Severn King' and
the 'Severn Queen' met
similar fates, one being
scrapped at Newport
and the other being cut
up at Sharpness. The
'Severn Princess',
however, had a
different fate ahead.
The last of the ferries
used from Beachley, it
was eventually taken to
Ireland and used as a
coastal freighter. In
1998 a local resident
found the ferry in
Kikieran harbour in a
dilapidated state, and
the people of Chepstow
rallied together to fund
her journey home. The
'Severn Princess' was in
need of extensive
restoration, which is still
going on - it has been
undertaken by the
'Severn Princess'
Restoration Group.

Chepstow, The River Severn Ferry 1936 87417
This is the 'Severn King' once more, this time taking on cars ready for the trip across the Severn. Note the cars (or should we say automobiles?) getting ready to drive onto the ferry. It is interesting that although it carries a Chepstow postmark, Beachley is on the English side of the Severn.

Chepstow, Town Gate 1936 87413
The photographer was positioned on Moor Street looking down towards the Town Gate. Note the unmarked roads, the shops on the left (D H Davies and M Woods) and the various forms of traffic (there are bicycles and motor cars, and a bus on the left). This area of the town is now much modernised, and also much busier.

Chepstow, The Bridge c1950 C77089
We are looking down onto the old bridge with the castle in the centre left of the picture. This bridge has now been superseded and replaced by a modern version. Note the double-decker bus entering Chepstow via the bridge.

◀ **Chepstow, Beaufort Square 1957** C77134 The tall building in the centre of the picture is the former Barclays Bank, since demolished. To the front of it we can see the war memorial. Across the street is a branch of F W Woolworth.

Chepstow, The Castle from the Bridge 1893 32495

The original castle on this site was begun by William FitzOsbern in 1067. He chose this particular location for its strategic position on a long, narrow ridge overlooking the river Wye. FitzOsbern built a long, rectangular fortified hall on the narrowest part of the ridge. This 'Great Tower' features pilasters and a string course of re-used Roman tiles. Its walls were surprisingly thin - about 3 to 6ft thick, as opposed to the norm of 8 to 20ft. The hall was in turn protected by a stone curtain wall on all four sides. On the landward side he added a ditch as a further defensive measure.

▼ Chepstow, View near Wyndcliffe 1959 C77156

With the Severn Estuary in the distance, this is an excellent view of the winding River Wye on its way to the coast.

◀ Chepstow, Welsh Street 1957 C77132

This photograph is taken from the Town Gate, looking up Welsh Street with Moor Street leading off to the left. Note the King's Head down Welsh Street on the left - it is still there today. It is interesting that its hanging sign now has a portrait of Charles I rather than the one of Henry VIII shown here.

Chepstow, High Street 1950 C77136
This view is much changed today. Lloyds Bank on the left is no longer there, and the National Provincial Bank further up on the left is now Barclays Bank, which has been altered extensively. Note also the war memorial, centre left.

Chepstow, High Street c1935 C77009
The shops on the left have not survived, and this view of the town has changed considerably over the years. Looking down the left-hand side of the street, we can see Edwards Confectioner, a printer's, a lending library and a shop advertising India and China tea. Note Skyrmes Café and Boarding House on the right and the ornate clock face.

Chepstow, The Town Centre 1936 87416
The buildings on both sides of the road have been extensively altered over the years. Note the Bush Hotel on the right (no longer trading). The hotel far down the street on the right is the Beaufort Hotel today.

▲ **Clydach**
General View 1936 87835
Perched on a steep hill, the photographer has done justice to this picturesque view just off the Heads of the Valleys Road. The village was the birthplace of Sir Bartle Frere (1815-84), the first High Commissioner of South Africa (1877). This view remains much the same today.

◀ **Clydach**
The Village c1965
C340012
Another picture of the village, this time taken from the other side of the gorge. The quarry seen in the top right of the picture is now disused, but the rest of the picture is little changed today. Many features of Clydach's industrial heyday are barely visible or vanished today, including quarries, limeworks, tramways, railways, bridges, works cottages, chapels and pubs.

Clydach Gorge

▼ **Clydach, Lower Fall 1893** 32603
This view of the river has changed somewhat today. It is now
a little overgrown with a campsite and picnic spot nearby.
Before its industrialisation the area would have been densely
wooded, but the combination of a plentiful supply of iron ore
limestone, wood for charcoal and water for power, made it
an ideal location for iron working, which came to the area in
the 17th century. In the 18th century the Clydach Ironworks
was built, and local coal measures supplied the necessary
coal for the production of coke, thereby relieving the
pressure on the local woodland. These coke-fired ironworks
were first fired in 1792 and for the last time in 1877, when
the company became bankrupt.

◄ **Clydach, The Wells
1893** 32605
There was still an
ironworks nearby at this
time, so it is possible
that the men and boys in
this photograph are from
there. Clydach Gorge is
half a mile in width and
over three and a half
miles in length, dropping
down from 1,100 feet
above sea level in the
west to 400 feet in the
east.

◄ **Gardiffaith, High Street c1955** G245009
This is an interesting view of the steeply-sloping High street. S Loveday & Co, 'Radio & Television & Electrical Contractors', is on the left, with shop assistant and passer-by looking at the camera. Above the shop front is an advertisement for Philips radios and televisions. Note also the two boys left and right, one intently staring at the camera, the other somewhat less interested.

Gardiffaith, General View c1955

G245002

An excellent view of a working village. It is perhaps understandable that Monmouthshire is so well known for its castles, monastic buildings and churches, but there is another side to the county -its industrial heritage. Note the man on the scaffolding and the two men looking under the bonnet of the car on the left of the picture (doubtless the mechanic is, by tradition, sucking in his breath and shaking his head at this point), and the various other vehicles.

Gardiffaith, Herberts Road c1955 G245020

Note the absence of road markings, the Co-operative shop on the left, and the various cars and passers-by.

Gilwern, The Village c1960 G246008

This view of the village is now much more densely overgrown. There are also many more buildings in this area of the village now, but the buildings pictured here still exist.

Gilwern, The Village c1955 G24701
This picture was taken from outside the Navigation Inn just off the Heads of the Valleys Road. The chapel of the Gilwern United Reformed Church (founded in 1885), in the centre of the picture, is much the same today as it is in the photograph. On the right, by the van, is now the site of the Bridgend Inn, standing above the point where the canal runs under the bridge.

Gilwern, The Canal c1960 G246005
The canal runs through Gilwern; it is very picturesque, and there are now moorings in Gilwern for pleasure boats outside the Bridgend Inn. This view was taken further along the canal.

Llandogo, River Wye c1955 L383023
The river Wye passes through some spectacular scenery and this is no exception. The Wye rises on Plynlimon in the Cambrian Mountains and flows into the Severn at Beachley Point near Chepstow.

▼ Llandogo, The Village c1955 L383032

This village is certainly set in an area of evident natural beauty. Note the bicyclist, the tricyclist (perhaps his younger brother?), and the rest of their party further along on the left. The garage opposite has the old-style petrol pumps. The Sloop Hotel is on the left.

▼ Llandogo, The Village c1955 L383042

This general view of the village gives us a clear picture of the village layout.

▲ Llandogo, Dorothy's Stores c1955 L383052
Opposite the stores we can see the warning sign for a school just before the parked car (something of an overreaction for the motorist - simply slowing down was probably what was wanted). The store advertises three brands of cigarette - Woodbine, Craven 'A' and Players Navy Cut.

◄ **Llanellen, The Church 1898** 41690
A very modest church this, by Monmouthshire standards. Note the heavily overgrown churchyard and the crenellated church tower. As well as serving as a means of calling the faithful to services by means of its bells, these towers also acted as vantage points in the event of war.

Govilon
Llanfoist Boathouse c1955 G247014
The boatyard in the picture was built c1815; it still exists. Boats can
be hired or moored here, and the building has been restored and is
now a house. It was once an iron-ore warehouse from which the
ore was loaded onto canal boats and shipped on to local ironworks.
There is still some evidence of this traffic in the form of tramlines.

Llanthony

The origins of the priory here date back, so the story goes, to c1100, when the Norman nobleman William de Lacy was hunting here on land owned by his brother. He sheltered in a ruined chapel dedicated to Dewi Sant (Saint David). The experience affected him sufficiently profoundly for him to renounce the world and become a contemplative hermit. After three years of solitude, he was joined by Emesius; the two men, together with their followers, decided to seek a life of contemplation and solitude together. They set about building a church, and the growing community became affiliated with the Austin (Augustinian) Canons. After a brief period of unrest with the native Welsh when the community was forced to relocate across the border, they returned in 1175 to resettle at Llanthony and build a new church. Caught as it was in the firing line of frequent border disputes, the priory was never destined to prosper, and it was eventually dissolved in 1538. In the 18th century part of the priory was converted into a shooting lodge, but it was the acquisition of the estate, including the remains of the priory, by Walter Savage Landor in 1807 which had the most telling effect. His extravagant plans included a school, 10,000 cedars of Lebanon and a population of Merino sheep; this put him at loggerheads with his tenants, and the huge expense led him into bankruptcy. The estate was assigned to trustees in 1815.

Llanthony, The Valley 1895 32612
The beautiful landscape and the tranquillity indicated in this view give us the reason why William de Lacy chose to renounce the world and live a life of contemplation here in c1100.

◄ **Llanthony, The Abbey from the North-West 1893** 32614
An atmospheric view of the ruined abbey and the surrounding hills. By the time Gerald of Wales, or Geraldus Cambrensis, came across it in 1188 in the course of his travels, he described it as roofed in 'sheets of lead and built of squared stones'. Of the monks, he wrote: 'They sit in their cloisters in this monastery breathing the fresh air and gaze up at distant prospects which rise above their own lofty rooftops and there they see as far as the eye can reach, mountain peaks which rise to meet the sky and often enough herds of wild deer which are grazing on the summits'.

Llanthony, The Abbey from the North-East 1893 32613

According to tradition, the church of David by the River Honddu described in the name 'Llandwi Nant Honddu' was established by Dewi Sant (Saint David), the patron saint of Wales, in the 6th century. This could have been the reason why the Norman knights, later to be Augustinian canons, chose this spot for meditation. Note the lady sporting an elaborate hat reclining in the centre foreground.

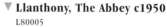

Llanthony, The Abbey c1950

L80005

The priory was completed within fifty years of its foundation, and managed to survive in this valley for the following three hundred years; then, together with so many of the country's other monasteries, it was suppressed during the Dissolution of the Monasteries by Henry VIII in 1539. In the following years the fabric of the abbey gradually decayed, but the infirmary and its chapel became the parish church.

Llanthony, The Abbey Hotel 1893 32617

The picturesque ruins eventually became an attraction for artists and poets in search of romantic inspiration, and in 1807 the abbey eventually came under the ownership of Walter Savage Landor, who arrived with great plans for the estate. Financial difficulties caused him to flee the country. In 1855 an Oxford professor wrote that the buildings were 'in utter ruin, its priory's house an inn which intrudes into the south-west tower of the church itself, its cloister a farmyard, its chapter house a calf-pen, ... so to speak in a state of nature'. Today the ruins are officially scheduled as an ancient monument under the care of CADW, the Welsh Historic Monuments Agency. The Abbey Hotel is still here, offering pony trekking and hotel accommodation.

◄ **Llanvetherine
The Village c1950**
L386002
On our way into the
village, we can see a
chapel on the left. Note
the unmarked road.

Llanvetherine

◀ **Llanvetherine, White Castle c1950** L386001
So named because it was once coated in white plaster,
White Castle was one of three - White, Skenfrith and
Grosmont - granted by King John to Hubert de Burgh in
1201. Together they are known as the 'Welsh Trilateral'.
With the exception of a brief period (1205-19, when they
were taken by William de Braose), the castles stayed in
the possession of de Burgh until he fell out of royal
favour in 1232, whereupon they all reverted to the
Crown.

◀ **Mardy, The Village
c1965** M282002
We are just entering the
village at the point where
the 30mph speed
restriction is displayed
on right and left. This
area is now very much a
part of the sprawl of
Abergavenny, although
in this picture it
resembles a small, quiet
village.

Mathern, The Palace 1906 54514
Once the home of the diocesan bishop, this fine Medieval building still survives as a testimony to the power of the church in the area in former times.

Mathern, The Church 1906 54515
This church is typical of the area, its distinctive tower fitting well into the picturesque setting.

Monmouth

The town has a long history. Built on the site of the Roman settlement of Blestium, Monmouth was also occupied by Norman settlers; William FitzOsbern established the first wooden fortress here. This was replaced in the 12th century by a more permanent stone structure. A settlement grew around the castle walls, including a Benedictine priory. Perhaps one of the more famous sons of the town is the 12th-century Geoffrey of Monmouth. Harry of Monmouth, later to become King Henry V, was born in the castle in 1387, and defeated the French in the Battle of Agincourt in 1415. The battle is also well-known for the formidable effect of the Welsh longbowmen, who, according to Shakespeare's 'Henry V', fought well for their King: 'Welshmen did good service ... wearing leeks in their Monmouth caps'.

Agincourt Square was once the site of the market place, and is now the centre of the town; it was so named to commemorate the great battle, and a statue of Henry V has stood in the square since 1792. The Shire Hall, which also stands in the square, has a long history. It was the place where in 1839 the Chartist John Frost and his companions were tried and condemned to death for their adherence to the Chartist cause - the sentence was later commuted to transportation. Another famous resident is also commemorated by a statue in the square: C S Rolls of the Rolls Royce Company lived nearby at Hendre until his death in a flying accident in 1910.

One of the unique attractions in Monmouth has to be the Monnow Bridge with its distinctive fortified gate. Originally a wooden structure (its remains have been found), the bridge is late Norman, built in 1262, and is one of the few such examples in Britain. Although impressively built to withstand attack, including the addition of a portcullis, the bridge proved ineffective: the River Monnow which it spanned can easily be forded, and during the Civil War this is exactly what happened, so that the defenders soon found themselves surrounded.

Monmouth has retained its medieval street layout, and this helps to give a distinctive feel to the historic town.

Monmouth, The Mill on the Monnow 1893 32516
This is a superb view of the mill. We can clearly see the mill race and weir. Note also the spire of the church in the centre of the picture.

Monmouth, The Backstone 1893 32518
This is a dramatic example of a stratified rock formation apparently teetering on the edge of a precipice and looking out over the valley beyond.

Monmouth
The Castle 1896 38693
The castle was built between 1067 and 1071 by William
FitzOsbern. By 1100 it had become an important place, one of a
chain of impressive fortresses intended to aid in the subjugation of
south-east Wales and to keep the 'troublesome Welsh' subjugated.
It is the seat of the Marcher Lordship of Monmouth. The 12th-
century holder of the title was William FitzBaderon, whose family
was to hold the lordship for over 150 years. Upon the death of the
last FitzBaderon, the title reverted to none other than Prince
Edward, son of King Henry III. The castle was once attacked and
briefly held by Simon de Montfort. When Edward became King, he
was to become famous for many things, though perhaps his
ruthless suppression of the Welsh would be his local epitaph. In
1267 the castle passed into the ownership of Edmund
Crouchback, the Earl of Lancaster. It was in this castle that the
future King Henry V was born in 1387.

Monmouth
The Shire Hall 1931
84581

The Shire Hall was built in 1724; the statue below the clock face is of Henry V, placed there in 1792. It was in this very hall that John Frost and his fellow Chartists were tried in 1839 - they were initially condemned to death, but this sentence was eventually commuted to transportation. The statue to the front of the building is of C S Rolls, one of the founders of the Rolls-Royce car company, who lived at nearby Hendre and was killed in a flying accident in 1910.

◀ **Monmouth**
The Bridge over the
Monnow 1891 28780
This gate is a Norman
structure dating from
1262, and it is a rare
example of a fortified
gateway on a bridge.
Note the spectator
eyeing the camera from
the centre of the bridge
and the buildings just
beyond the gate with the
hanging sign reading
'Vaults'. These buildings
were subsequently
removed to make way
for the Barley Mow.

Monmouth, Cindrell Street 1939 M91038
The building on the right is the Overmonnow Post Office, advertising a Parcel Post service and with the built-in post box to the left of the window. Note also the hanging sign on the left advertising the Rising Sun.

Monmouth The Old Gate c1950 M91037
The gate incorporates a fine example of a Norman arch. Note also the church partly concealed by the signpost on the left. Note the Barley Mow's hanging sign through the arch.

Monmouth The Monnow Bridge Gate 1939 M91041
By this time the Vaults have disappeared to make way for the Barley Mow.

▼ **Monmouth, St Thomas Square 1939** M91035
The monument opposite the Green Dragon Inn in the centre of the
picture is now in the centre of a busy roundabout. St Thomas's church
on the right has been much restored, but it retains both its Norman
choir arch and north door dating from the early 12th century.

▼ **Monmouth, Agincourt Square 1914** 67634
This square is so named in commemoration of Henry V's victory at Agincourt in
1415. Henry of Monmouth, who was to be crowned King Henry V of England, was
born in the castle in 1387. The church spire rising over the rooftops is that of St
Mary's. Note the curious policeman evidently waiting patiently for some traffic to
direct. Note also the various shops (reading left to right): Bowers 'Noted Sweet
Shop', Yearsley, the Monmouth Tobacconist, a hairdressing salon, Monmouth
House, and W Hughes, Outfitter. A sign over the portico (left) directs people to the
cinema.

▲ **Monmouth, Agincourt
Square 1931** 84583a
We are looking into
Agincourt Square from a
different angle. The spire
of St Mary's overshadows
the busy street scene.
Note the Schweppes
delivery truck on the left.

◄ **Monmouth**
The Grammar School 1896 38689
The street to the front of the school buildings is so quiet that two gentlemen can be perfectly relaxed strolling down the middle of the road. The school itself is still here, offering boarding and day schooling for boys aged 7 to 18. A commemorative plaque outside the school reads 'Monmouth School. On this site William Jones, citizen and haberdasher of London founded this school in AD 1615. The original schoolhouse was demolished AD 1865 and these buildings erected. The first stone being laid by the Master of the Worshipful Company of Haberdashers. This entrance was closed in 1961 upon replacement by the adjoining wrought iron gates salvaged from the Haberdashers Hall in the City of London destroyed by enemy action AD 1941. Serve and Obey'.

Pontymister

Pontymister, Gelli Crescent c1950 P309002
On the left we can see a long row of terraced
workers' cottages. Note the man with his handcart
along the right-hand side of the road and the
delivery truck on the left.

◄ **Pontymister
Canal Bridge and
Mariah Hill c1955**
P309006
This peaceful stretch of
the canal leads us
towards the Prince of
Wales public house. The
stone-built Mariah
Bridge leads to
Rosemont Avenue.

**Pontymister
Ty-Isaf c1955** P309003
The road in front of the houses is Channel View, and beneath it we can see the railway lines, now only a single main line used primarily to transport coils from the Llanwern steelworks to the Ebbw Vale steelworks for processing.

**Pontymister
Twm Barlwm from the Canal c1955** P309007
Another view of the canal, showing how overgrown it had become by this time. Note the bollard strategically placed in the centre of the towpath, presumably to prevent vehicular access.

**Pontymister
View from Ochwyth c1955** P309008
This photograph gives us some idea of the rural setting for this village, something of a contrast to the dense housing of the village itself.

◄ **Portskewett
The Village Green
1931** P311012
This photograph stands
as a reminder of quieter
days in the village.
Unfortunately, the
increased use of the
motor car throughout
the 20th century saw the
demise of this kind of
rural scene in many
villages around Wales.

◄ Portskewett
The Village 1931
P311010

This view has not changed much in the intervening years, but note the absence of road markings. Although the road width and traffic flow has changed, the buildings are distinctive and easily recognisable today.

▼ Portskewett
The Stocks c1930 P311013

This form of punishment was once commonplace but very few original sets of stocks exist today. In a village where everyone knew everyone else - and each other's business - the effect of a day in the stocks must have been considerable. There are sufficient holes to accommodate three wrongdoers at a time - this would probably have constituted a crime wave!

◄ Rockfield, The Bridge
1893 32524

The stone bridge pictured here was washed away in a flood in c1957; it was replaced by a steel construction built onto the stone footings of the previous bridge.

Raglan

Raglan Castle is probably one of the most majestic castles in Wales. Set upon a ridge amidst a wondrous landscape, it has cast an impressive shadow over the area for centuries. Like most Norman structures, the castle was the successor of a motte and bailey fortification. Raglan was granted to Walter Bloet by Earl Richard de Clair of Chepstow around 1174, and in return Bloet had to provide the earl with military assistance. Raglan remained in the Bloet family until the mid 15th century. Then it passed into the hands of William ap Thomas, a member of the minor Welsh gentry, who began to build the castle as we see it today.

Following the death of William ap Thomas in 1445, the castle passed into the hands of his eldest son, another William, who took the surname Herbert. It was this William Herbert and his family who were entrusted to bring up the young Henry Tudor (later Henry VII) at Raglan. Herbert was to rise to the position of earl of Pembroke, thus becoming one of the first members of the Welsh gentry to rise in the English peerage. This rise enabled Herbert to continue with the building of the castle at Raglan on a grand scale, although he did not have

Raglan, The Castle, the South Side and the Keep 1893 32534
William Herbert's tower-keep rises on the right of this picture. The building was designed to incorporate the latest in military architectural thinking. The castle is plainly more of a military stronghold than a stately home - the keep was even separated from the rest of the castle by its own moat and double drawbridge

much time to enjoy his work. In 1469 earl William and his brother were defeated at the battle of Edgecote by the earl of Warwick, Richard Neville the 'kingmaker', who swiftly had the men executed.

Raglan was at its height in the Elizabethan period, when the visiting poet Thomas Churchyard wrote 'The Worthines of Wales' (1587):

'Not farre from thence, a famous Castle fine,
That Raglan hight, stands moted almost round:
Made of freestone, upright as straight as line,
Whose workmanship, in beautie doth abound.
The curious knots, wrought all with edged toole,
The stately Tower, that looks ore pond and poole:
The Fountain trim, that runs both day and night,
Doth Yeeld in showe, a rare and noble sight.'

The civil wars would ruin Churchyard's fine castle forever. During the years running up to 1646, the castle was a stronghold for Royalist forces and was visited several times by King Charles himself. In 1646 the castle was besieged by Parliamentarian troops under the command of Colonel Thomas Morgan, but it held out against him well. By August, however, the siege works had reached within 60 yards of the castle, and Henry Somerset, who commanded the garrison, decided to surrender. Along with the sustained damage that the siege caused to the castle, it was deliberately damaged by the Parliamentarians, including the destruction of a fine library collection. An account states that 'afterwards it was demolished, and the lead and timber carried off to Monmouth'.

The castle was allowed to fall apart following the Civil Wars; much of the interior was salvaged by the locals, and several items have duly shown up later. Today the care of the castle and site is entrusted into the hands of CADW, the Welsh Historic Monuments Service.

Raglan
The Castle c1900 R3336
William Herbert remodelled Raglan in the contemporary French style with multi-angular towers and ornate machicolations. Also a professional soldier, William Herbert had fought for and been knighted by Henry VI. Herbert surpassed even the lofty achievement of knighthood when he supported Edward IV at Mortimer's Cross in 1461. For this act he was awarded the title of Baron Herbert. Note the seated man and boy watching the camera. There is now a path leading up to the gatehouse, and the building has had the damaging ivy removed.

Raglan, The Castle 1906 54518
Herbert also went on to be made Knight of the Garter in 1462. In 1468 he was to become Earl of Pembroke as a reward for taking Harlech Castle and taking captive Jasper Tudor and Prince Henry (later Henry VII).

▼ **Raglan, The Castle, the Fountain Court 1893** 32532
The castle was divided into two courts: the Stone Court and the Fountain Court.
They are separated from one another by a building that included the great hall, the
earl's private dining room, a buttery, a withdrawing room and the great gallery. The
Fountain Court was the site of the castle's state apartments.

◀ **Raglan**
The Castle,
Grand Staircase
1914 67692
Raglan was the
last castle to hold
out against
Parliament in
1646. On his
restoration,
Charles II
rewarded the
Pembroke family
by raising it from
an earldom to a
marquessate. In
the 17th century,
the second
marquess wrote a
treatise on the use
of steam and
water-power in
which he
anticipated the
invention of the
steam-pump.

▲ **Raglan, The Castle 1893**
32533
One famous visitor, Charles
I, arrived at the castle on 3
July from Abergavenny,
after his defeat at the hands
of the New Model Army at
Naseby on 14 June 1645.
The king was still in
residence when the news
came that Goring had been
defeated at Langport by
Fairfax and Cromwell. The
ivy is no more, for which
the stonework and future
generations of appreciative
visitors can be thankful.
Note the table and benches
in the centre foreground.

◀ **Raglan**
The Castle 1906 54517
This excellent view of the castle shows the manicured lawns and hedging off-setting the ivy-clad walls on the left. Note that only a mere thirteen years after 32533 was taken, we can see a distinct improvement in the upkeep of the remains of the castle. Today's visitors are no longer allowed access to the walkway above the gateway (note the safety railings). A variety of public events are held in the grounds.

Raglan, The Beaufort Arms Hotel 1914 67685c
This hotel has now been extensively modernised and looks different today. Some of the trees have also been removed over the intervening years. The hotel is mentioned in the 1901 Kelly's Directory when the proprieter was Thames Leech. Also mentioned is Robert Ferrett, job master at Beaufort Arms yard.

Raglan, Beaufort Square 1914 67685
On the left of the picture is the war memorial. Note the man and child walking away from the camera in the centre of the photograph.

Raglan
High Street 1914 67686
The shops on the right are still in existence. Note the children
sitting on the step on the right. This building has since been
demolished, but we gather planning permission is being sought to
replace it. The coach house doorway further up on the right is now
the site of a fish and chip shop. Note also the billboards leaning up
against the wall on the right, and the sign reading 'Refreshment
Rooms'. We can also just see the tin roof of a building on the left
beyond the first cottage. One local resident remembers the locals
using it as a place to hang out washing to dry on rainy days. The
cobbled pavements have also long since disappeared.

**Raglan
High Street 1914**
67687
The tower of St Cadoc's can be seen behind the buildings on the right. The church is built of stone in the early Perpendicular style and was restored in 1868. Note also the upturned bicycle outside Davies and Jones Bicycle shop on the right. The Ship Hotel, on the left, boasts an ancient fireplace, said to originate from Raglan Castle.

Raglan
The Church Cross
1914 67690
Unfortunately, the cross in the churchyard of St Cadoc's pictured here appears to have met with an accident and has been smashed; it is also somewhat overgrown with ivy. This and other pictures of it are all that remain to show it as it was.

◀ Raglan, The Village 1906 54520

Raglan was (and still is, thank goodness) the charming village pictured here. In the centre of the photograph is the parish church of St Cadoc with its distinctive tower.

▼ Raglan, Chepstow Road 1914 67683

The cottage which the man (the local postman?) is either entering or leaving is still in existence. The tower of St Cadoc's is in the centre of the photograph. The school building on the right is now next to a more modern school; its bell tower has been removed. The cobbled pavements on the left have also been removed in favour of modern paving.

◀ Raglan, Castle Street 1914 67684

This photograph appears to have been taken from the site of the memorial to the dead of the two World Wars, although it would obviously not have been present at the time this photograph was taken. The tree-lined walkway on the left in front of the Beaufort Arms still exists. Note the refreshment rooms (now a house) on the right, and the boy in shorts in the centre of the photograph. Note also the water pump and trough on the left of the picture beneath the trees.

Tintern

The abbey at Tintern has long been a place of beauty and fascination for visitors. Founded in 1131, it was the first Cistercian monastery in Wales, a product of the order's rapid move across Europe from their beginnings in France. Walter fitz Richard of Clare was the founder of the White Monks' abbey, choosing the new order over the more well-known Black Monks, the Benedictines, who had been in Wales for some time. Nestled in their little valley, the community continued to grow throughout the 12th century, gaining patronage and cultivating the land.

By the 13th century, extensive building had begun to take place. By the beginning of the 14th century the abbey was at its height, although in this period problems arose which were to have serious consequences on the future of the abbey. One of the most serious was the Black Death, which robbed the area of many of the hands that were needed to cultivate the abbey's now extensive lands. Also, the uprising of Owain Glyndwr had a detrimental effect - some of the abbey's buildings were damaged by the Welsh rebels. The end of the abbey came with Henry VIII's Dissolution of the

Tintern, General View 1893 32460
The Abbey ruins are centre right of the picture. Note the narrow bridge crossing the river, which still exists.

Monasteries; it eventually surrendered to its fate in September 1536. All the remaining possessions of the abbey were catalogued and sent to the king's treasury.

It was not until the 18th century that Tintern began to attract tourists. The Romantic period saw the abbey fast becoming the jewel in the crown of the Wye valley. Men were employed to clear away two centuries of debris to reveal the buildings, if not in their former glory, at least with a view toward preservation. Visits were made by the artist J M W Turner, who sketched the abbey and later produced some wonderful watercolours of it, and by the poet William Wordsworth, who wrote 'Lines Composed a Few Miles Above Tintern Abbey'. Of this poem he said that 'No poem of mine was composed under circumstances more pleasant for me to remember than this'; Wordsworth's writings did much to promote the area in 'romantic' circles, and visitors flocked to the abbey. The 19th century, with the building of a new road past the site, saw a continued flow of visitors, and the abbey became one of the foremost attractions in Wales. In 1901 the abbey was recognised as a monument of national importance, and was purchased by the Crown. Work began on the repair and preservation of the ruins, and by 1928 the Daily Telegraph could announce that restoration work on the abbey was nearly complete. In 1984 the site came under the control of CADW, Welsh Historic Monuments, who continue to look after the abbey today.

Tintern Abbey c1872 6358
A very atmospheric view of the abbey ruins, complete with beached fishing smack. Note the slip-way (centre right), now no longer there.

Tintern, The Abbey, from the South-West 1893 32468
The south-west wall is being renovated at the time of writing. The present remains were built in the decorated style between 1270 and 1301.

Tintern Abbey 1890 27587
This truly splendid view shows the abbey ruins and the busy pastoral scene surrounding it. The white buildings in the centre of the photograph are where the thirsty tourist can find the Anchor Tea-Rooms. There is also now a Visitors' Centre here to serve the large numbers of visitors to the abbey. The ivy has since been removed, and there is a programme of preservation underway.

◄ **Tintern
The Chapel 1893**
32480
This chapel is sited just
above the abbey ruins,
which we can just see in
the centre of the picture
beyond and below the
church tower. The tower
has since been removed.

◀ **Tintern, The Abbey
The Nave 1893** 32476
This haunting picture shows
the deep mouldings and
intricate architectural details
of the abbey. The central
area would have been used
as the lay brothers' choir,
and screen walls would have
divided off the aisles at the
north and south. The doors
in the bottom of the far wall
are no longer in place.

▼ **Tintern, The Village
1893** 32461
The ruins of the abbey
are visible in the
distance. This
photograph shows how
Tintern nestles in
amongst the surrounding
hills.

◀ **Tintern
The Village 1893** 32478
The photographer is
being closely observed
by the man looking over
the railings on the left of
the picture.

Tintern, The Village 1925 76881
Although tourism has been important to the village for the last 200 years, other local industries included forestry, farming and from the mid 16th century to the end of the 19th century, wine making. This charming view of the village comes complete with horse and cart in the centre left of the picture. This could almost be a still from a period drama film set. Note the Rose & Crown 'Private' Hotel on the left, which carries on today as a public house (minus the ivy).

Undy

Undy, The Village c1950 U63014

Undy has a long history: it was settled by the Romans from AD43 to AD410. A church was founded here by St Dubritus in AD512, dedicated to St Gwyndaf and his wife Wyndaf. As Undy is 'Gwindi' in Welsh, some think that this could be the origin of the village name. The current church of St Mary is built on the same spot as the original church. In this view we see a quiet, rural crossroads, evidently not over-burdened in terms of traffic. The shop on the left is the Bon Bon - many villages had this type of wooden shop in the 1950s.

Undy, The Village c1950 U63016

This view shows the village from the opposite direction from U63014. Several limestone quarries provided work for the locals during the 19th century, although farming has always been important. In Kelly's Directory of 1901, the commercial section lists a butcher, a bailiff, a carpenter and wheelwright, a molecatcher and 19 farmers.

Usk

Usk is a small picturesque town set on the banks of the river from which it takes its name, and is spread over the site of the Roman Burrium, a predecessor of Caerleon. Although the main expansion period of the town took place during the 18th and 19th centuries, the town was founded around a Norman castle. Built in the 12th century, Usk Castle belonged to the De Clares and the earls of March, and was captured by Simon de Montfort in 1265. The ruins are today in private hands; they include a keep, a round tower and a gatehouse, some parts dating back to the castle's Norman origins, and some parts altered in the 15th century.

Dating from around 1100, the church in Usk was dedicated to St Mary, and became a Benedictine nunnery re-founded by Richard de Clare, son of 'Strongbow', in the 13th century. The church has many unique features. One of them is a brass plaque with a very early Welsh inscription, possibly the earliest inscription in brass in the Welsh dialect, dating from around 1400. By the 18th century Usk was becoming well known for its japanned ware, and this lifted the town to new economic heights. Many of the buildings in the town were modernised during this period, and it is this that gives the town its distinctive atmosphere. Today Usk is home to many fine buildings; it also houses the Rural Life Museum, set up to portray what it would have been like to live in the town during past times.

Usk
The Castle c1955 U59007
Now inaccessible to members of the public (it stands in private grounds), the castle stands on a spur overlooking the town. The first post-Roman defences to be built on the site were probably in place soon after 1066, but the castle itself was started in 1138, with many improvements made over the next two centuries.

**Usk, St Mary's Church ▶
c1960** U59018
This church was once the chapel of a Benedictine nunnery founded by Richard de Clare, son of 'Strongbow', in 1236. The obelisk on the right is a memorial to James Williams 'of this Town 1810-1863' and his wife Elizabeth, who died in 1875.

▼ Usk, The Riverside c1960
U59035
Here we see Conigar Walk running down the bank of the River Usk. We can also see the old railway bridge crossing the river in the centre of the photograph in the distance; and it is still to be found here, albeit disused.

▲ Usk, The Bridge and Conigar Walk c1960
U59036
The road bridge crosses the Usk at this point. Both these views of the river have changed thanks to the installation of flood defence systems which have increased the height of the banks on either side, but it is still a pretty spot for a stroll along the riverbank. Note the woman out for a walk on Conigar Walk.

◀ **Usk, The Three Salmons Hotel c1965** U59078
The Three Salmons Hotel, which stands on the A471 to Abergavenny, looks much the same today, except that it has now expanded to occupy the premises across the road. The hanging sign sporting the three salmons on the corner of the building has now been removed, presumably to allow for the higher vehicles which use this road.

Old Monmouthshire

Over the centuries, Monmouthshire has undergone many boundary changes, the most significant of which came during the 19th and 20th centuries. The onset of industrialisation in the south Wales valleys brought about change which affected the very fabric of life there. For the first time, workers no longer had to rely on the weather or the seasons for their fortunes. Industrialisation meant stable wages and stable jobs and many people left their traditional occupations in the country for new opportunities in the towns that had sprung up with industrialisation.

The new towns were dangerous places to be, however, made up as they were of largely male populations. Blaenafon and Nant Y Glo typified this 'new frontier'. As the formerly rural workers eventually settled down to their unfamiliar roles in those towns and others, they began to feel they could safely bring their wives and children in from the countryside to join them. That safety was somewhat illusory, however, and was often disturbed by riots and insurrection. The most notable of these was at

Abertillery, Foundry Bridge c1955 A279052
Situated on the western extremities of what was once the county of Monmouthshire, Abertillery is very much a typical Welsh industrial town. In the early 20th century it was the second largest town in the county. This view shows the terraced housing so common in the valleys. Note the bus with the split windscreen advertising the services of Cyril Rogers.

Newport in 1839, when the Chartists under John Frost and William Jones stormed a garrison of 'Redcoats' at The Westgate Hotel, leading to the transportation of the ringleaders. This story is dramatised in the book 'Rape of the Fair Country' by Alexander Cordell, which also well-depicts life in industrial Monmouthshire in the early 1800s.

The Monmouthshire of today is much changed, principally by the boundary reviews of 1974. The photographs that follow are a glimpse of some of the towns and villages that were, for many years, an integral part of Monmouthshire; we hope you enjoy them.

Abertillery
The New Bridge c1955 A279012
This view of the bridge from the opposite side better illustrates the distinctive architectural style of the south Wales valleys - rows of identical terraces ascending the hillside. Before 1840 the area had been mainly rural, but a coal industry was already in place by 1850, when the railway arrived. Boom time came at the turn of the century. Between 1891 and 1911, the population rose from 10,846 to 35,415 owing to the influx of people seeking work in the local coal mines.

Cwmtillery, Mine Buildings c1955 C550036
Miners' cottages overlook the buildings and railway lines associated with the colliery at Cwmtillery, which opened in 1850. This area, however, was already occupied at a much earlier date - a Bronze Age axe was found at a settlement at Llanerch Padarn higher up the valley. The colliery finally closed in 1982.

Bedwas, Newport Road and the Square c1960 B475013
The poster on the extreme right of this picture is advertising the forthcoming local District Council elections. This has obviously not caused too much of a stir in sleepy Bedwas. Even the dogs are nonplussed - and the fact that they are happily standing in the middle of the road suggests that any traffic hazard in such a quiet backwater was probably very limited. The road works warned of by the sign were never likely to be the cause of too many traffic jams when car ownership was still quite low and the availability and use of public transport correspondingly high.

Bedwas
Newport Road c1960 B475019

Co-operative stores sprang up everywhere in places like Bedwas to bring affordable shopping to the valley areas, where they were often the main or only source of groceries and goods. The Co-ops were set up in conjunction with the workers (hence their name). Note the women catching up on all the gossip outside the shop, and the boy resting from the strains of pushing his wheelbarrow. The few aerials on the chimneys in Newport Road show that TV ownership - or rental - had made little impact by 1960. What other services that we now take for granted might have just arrived via the large recently covered trench in the road?

Caerleon
Castle Ruins and Usk Bridge 1931 C4003

Caerleon is a town of Roman origin. The Romans built a fortress here in c75AD and named it 'Isca', from the name of the River Usk. This to the Welsh became 'Caerleon', a corruption of 'Castra Legionis' or the 'Fort of the Legion'. The permanent legion was the 2nd Augustan, numbering between 5 and 6 thousand men. The first castle was a basic earthwork and wooden affair and was replaced in around 100AD by a more permanent stone structure. On the right hand side of the photograph is the sole remaining tower of the Norman Caerleon castle, next to what is now the Hanbury Arms, originally a 16th-century house. This tranquil scene is a far cry from the traffic thundering by on the M4 motorway just a short distance away today.

Caerleon, Priory Gateway 1931 C4002
This view of the somewhat overgrown and slightly tumbledown gateway of Caerleon Priory belies the fact that the impressive building beyond, which dates back to 1180 and which was originally a monastery and later a nunnery, is now a hotel of some distinction. The Priory itself was allegedly built on the site of Roman stables. The hotel's ready access from the M4 motorway means that the peaceful scene in this photograph must long since be a thing of the past. How times change!

Caerleon, Chapel 1899 43662
This picture shows some of Caerleon's distinctive buildings, the confident Victorian architecture contrasting sharply with the more humble dwellings on the right. Note the unmetalled road, which would have made travelling at the turn of the century hazardous and extremely mucky after rain!

Caerleon
The Roman Amphitheatre 1954 C4030
This structure would have provided the entertainment centre for the 2nd Augustan legion and is claimed to be the best-preserved amphitheatre in Britain. Capable of seating all 6,000 men of the garrison, it must have formed an impressive structure when completed in c80-100 AD. There are eight entrances to the amphitheatre, six for spectators and two for performers, the latter being the most elaborate. There are also traces of the small waiting rooms and stone benches used by the entertainers of the day, who must have been thankful for the lack of lions in rural Monmouthshire! Arthurian legend touched this place, as so many in Wales, for it has been known as King Arthur's Round Table since the Middle Ages. Much of the stone was plundered for construction over the centuries and can be found in buildings all over Caerleon.

**Caerleon
The Village 1893**

32642

This is a grand view of the River Usk, which winds its way through Caerleon. The solitary horse-drawn carriage in the middle of the road hints at quieter, perhaps gentler times, even if life was in many ways harsher too. A well-developed town for the time of this picture, it also shows the magnificent rural surroundings, as yet unencroached upon by 20th century development.

◀ **Crumlin, Viaduct 1893** 32647
Built to carry the Taff Vale Extension railway across the Ebbw and Kendon valleys to join the Taff Vale and Newport, Abergavenny and Hereford railways together, the 200 foot-high Crumlin viaduct was a 19th-century testimony to the economic power of coal. Designed by Thomas Kennard, the eight-pier viaduct was constructed by Charles Liddell, using castings from Falkirk and wrought iron from nearby Blaenavon. Construction began in 1853 and was finished in 1855, although the viaduct only came into service a year and half later. Demolished after the 1964 closure of the railway it carried, the elegant structure now exists only in photographs such as this.

Caerleon, The Square and War Memorial c1930 C4020

Perhaps the two cars here were the first motor vehicles in Caerleon. The one with the hard roof would definitely be better-suited to the Welsh climate. Such pictures bring home to us, from our 21st century vantage point, how much the car has come to dominate such everyday scenes, with yellow lines, traffic signs, lights and roundabouts. Note the small shops and the war memorial with its built-in drinking fountain. Is that Caerleon's first - and only - streetlight directly behind the memorial?

Cwm, Town Centre c1960
C517041

A typical town photograph, with the Co-op men's outfitters at the centre next to the more traditional smaller shops. The architecture of the Co-op shows the wealth of the industry in the area. Note the grand rooftop confidently displaying the words 'Ebbw Vale Industrial Provident Society Limited' - founded in 1899 - as if it would be there forever.

Cwmbran, c1955
C547009

Cwmbran itself is described as a 'New Town' although there are several places of historical note in the vicinity, such as the 12th-century Cistercian Abbey at Llantarnam. This picture again emphasises the rural beauty of the old county, as opposed to the better-known and aesthetically less appealing industrial views of south Wales.

▼ Cwmcarn, The Park and Memorial 1954 C548020

These memorials, found in nearly every town in both England and Wales, tell of the terrible consequences of the two World Wars to the small communities from which the men named on them were drawn. This figure, head bowed and rifle turned upside down, is a common sight.

▼ Ebbw Vale, The Roundabout c1955 E176018

This picture captures a Welsh community in the decade between the end of the war and the 'Swinging Sixties'. To the right of the picture is a railway stop signal; the front would have been coloured red with a white stripe, and the back white with a black stripe. The Ebbw valley lost its passenger service in 1962 when Dr Beeching made significant cuts, although the freight service continued to operate. Recently there have been plans to re-introduce a passenger service to Cardiff and Newport. It is hoped the service will help to ease the pressures of social exclusion and unemployment partly caused by Corus' closure of the Ebbw Valley Steelworks, and provide alternative transport for those in an area of low car ownership.

▲ Ebbw Vale
The Old Arch c1960
E176079

Children have been playing near railway lines for generations and the temptations of two lines so close together were obviously too much for the determined (probably) small boys who prised the railings apart to get to the embankment on the left of the picture. The dilapidated fence on the right would have been no obstacle to their hair-raising adventures, in a more innocent age, as what appears to be a well-worn path leading to the tunnel parapet and beyond suggests.

◄ **Ebbw Vale, General View c1955** E176036

Like so many of the valley towns, Ebbw Vale owed its existence to heavy industry. Steel making and mining helped to shape the town, and this picture captures beautifully the bustling atmosphere of industrial Wales in the 1950s: the works in the background, the railways transporting the goods in and out in the foreground, and the row upon row of workers' terraced houses rising steeply up the banks of the valley. How very different this view looks today, now that the 'smokestack industries' that powered the area have gone. Even the steelworks was re-landscaped to house the Garden Festival of Wales in 1992 - it is now a retail park.

**Newport
The Transporter
Bridge 1906** 54935a
Newport's most famous
landmark, the
transporter bridge (or
aerial ferry), was
opened in 1906. In the
latter half of the 18th
century the east bank of
the River Usk had been
developed, and a new
structure was needed to
link it with the west
bank. The low level of
the banks on either side
and the high tidal range
meant that conventional
bridge designs were not
practical, and so
Haynes and Arnodin
engineered a bridge
that could be operated
without obstructing
shipping - one of only
five such structures in
the world.

Newport, Commercial Street 1893 32629
The trams in the picture would soon give way to the new motor buses as road transport underwent yet another revolution. It is interesting to contrast the differences between Newport and some of the other turn-of-the-century pictures included in this section. Newport would have been the centre of fashionable Monmouthshire. The buildings here reflect its wealth as a port town, although the town's roots go back to the Norman period when a motte-and-bailey structure was built in the 12th century. The familiar pattern of its replacement by a stone structure followed soon after, and it was not long before a trading centre was established called 'Novus Burgus' or 'Castell Newydd', reflected in the city's contemporary Welsh name of 'Cas Newydd'.

Newport, The Bridge 1893 32630
This bridge over the River Usk is situated near the site of the old castle. It is famous for the Newport cherubs that adorn it - and also for the association with Houdini, who jumped into the river from its parapet in 1913. Here, the Usk is tidal, a feature which greatly assisted in the development of the port.

Newport, On the Canal 1896 38708
This flight of locks is probably on the Brecon and Monmouthshire canal, which was built between 1797 and 1812 for transporting stone from Brecon to Newport for export, and for moving processed lime from Talybont on Usk. The valleys' canal systems developed throughout the late 18th and early 19th centuries, and led to the development of Newport as a port. By the end of the 18th century it had become the principal coal port in south Wales; all this from what half a century before had been little more than a few wharves.

Newport, Westgate Square N25112
The town has not always been as peaceful as this picture suggests. In the 13th century it was seized by Simon de Montfort, and it was also sacked during the revolution of Owain Glyndwr in the 15th century. Industrialisation brought fresh tension, and in 1839 the town was the scene of Chartist riots led by John Frost. A large demonstration was held, which turned violent when soldiers confronted crowds close by the Westgate Hotel. The demonstrators eventually fled, leaving Frost to face execution. His sentence was eventually commuted to transportation.

Pontypool, The Grotto c1960 P126016
The grotto in Pontypool park was believed to have been the home of an old hermit, and is considered by academics to be the most important example in Wales. Around 1830 Molly Hanbury, the wife of one of the most successful ironmasters in the country, commissioned the decoration of the grotto with shells, crystals and bones. Today this charming structure is known as the Shell Grotto, but in 1960 it was clearly awaiting restoration.

◄ **Risca, The Canal from Darren Bridge c1955** R328010
Many places in south Wales have this dual identity, held in tension between the rural and the industrial. Here we see a marriage of the two: industrialisation brought about the canals, but when they were made redundant by the development of the faster and cheaper rail systems, many canals were abandoned, becoming a quiet part of the countryside. The women in the picture are taking advantage of this literal backwater to enjoy a walk in one of Wales' many beauty spots.

◄ Risca, Dan-y-Graig Road c1955 R328005
Situated north-west of Newport, Risca is a typical valley community. There were lime kilns at Dan-y-Graig, where a Roman lead mine was also discovered. In our post-industrial age you can now follow the same road out of Risca to the Dan-y-Graig nature reserve, which is situated on land given to the Gwent Wildlife Trust by the Risca Mineworkers Flower Show Society in 1987.

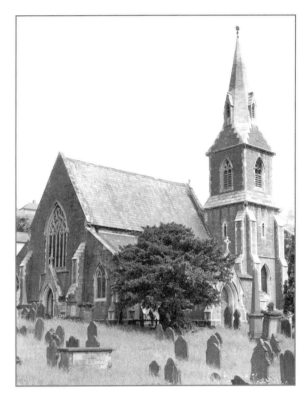

Risca, St Mary's Church c1955 R328032 ▲
Although the church you see here can be traced back to 1853, when it was dedicated by the Bishop of Llandaff, there have been churches on the site for far longer. As well as a memorial in the chancel from 1775, the church also has an Elizabethan chalice, and its bell dates from the 18th century. The earlier church had a Norman tower, but was demolished to make way for the present church, with its grander Victorian steeple. With the loss of so much industry in the area and the gradual drift from the church by an increasingly secular society, churches like St Mary's today struggle to remain viable.

◄ Tredegar, c1955 T265034
Although pig iron was being produced in the area in the late 18th century, it was the setting up of the Tredegar Iron Works in 1800 that gave the town prosperity, growth and its name. In 1801 the population was 619, but by 1811 it had reached 2,200. In 1850 3,000 men were employed at the works. This view overlooking the town provides a classic view of industrial Wales, with the terraced houses and industrial workings which so typified the 19th century. Just a few years after this picture was taken only waste tips were to be seen. In common with many similar communities, the people of Tredegar lost their livelihoods when the industries on which they depended were closed down.

Tredegar
Castle Street c1955 T265064

Tredegar believes its clock tower, the feature for which it is best known, to be unique. Built in 1858 for £1,000, the idea for the clock is believed to have come from a Mrs Davis, wife of the manager of the Tredegar Ironworks, who donated £400 towards its construction. Sadly, Mrs Davis died before she could raise the rest of the money needed to build the tower, but her husband contributed it anyway - perhaps as his memorial to his wife. The tower carries inscriptions on its four sides, including a dedication to 'Wellington, England's Hero'. The tower was designed and constructed by the engineer James Watson and is a fitting monument to the town's foundation and dependence on iron. The four clockfaces were originally lit by gas, but electricity took over and the tower underwent extensive restoration in the 1990s to maintain its prominence and preserve its significance to the heritage of Tredegar.

Index

Frith Book Co Titles

www.francisfrith.co.uk

The Frith Book Company publishes over 100 new titles each year. A selection of those currently available are listed below. For latest catalogue please contact Frith Book Co.

Town Books 96 pages, approx 100 photos. County and Themed Books 128 pages, approx 150 photos (unless specified). All titles hardback laminated case and jacket except those indicated pb (paperback)

Amersham, Chesham & Rickmansworth (pb)			Derby (pb)	1-85937-367-4	£9.99
	1-85937-340-2	£9.99	Derbyshire (pb)	1-85937-196-5	£9.99
Ancient Monuments & Stone Circles	1-85937-143-4	£17.99	Devon (pb)	1-85937-297-x	£9.99
Aylesbury (pb)	1-85937-227-9	£9.99	Dorset (pb)	1-85937-269-4	£9.99
Bakewell	1-85937-113-2	£12.99	Dorset Churches	1-85937-172-8	£17.99
Barnstaple (pb)	1-85937-300-3	£9.99	Dorset Coast (pb)	1-85937-299-6	£9.99
Bath (pb)	1-85937419-0	£9.99	Dorset Living Memories	1-85937-210-4	£14.99
Bedford (pb)	1-85937-205-8	£9.99	Down the Severn	1-85937-118-3	£14.99
Berkshire (pb)	1-85937-191-4	£9.99	Down the Thames (pb)	1-85937-278-3	£9.99
Berkshire Churches	1-85937-170-1	£17.99	Down the Trent	1-85937-311-9	£14.99
Blackpool (pb)	1-85937-382-8	£9.99	Dublin (pb)	1-85937-231-7	£9.99
Bognor Regis (pb)	1-85937-431-x	£9.99	East Anglia (pb)	1-85937-265-1	£9.99
Bournemouth	1-85937-067-5	£12.99	East London	1-85937-080-2	£14.99
Bradford (pb)	1-85937-204-x	£9.99	East Sussex	1-85937-130-2	£14.99
Brighton & Hove(pb)	1-85937-192-2	£8.99	Eastbourne	1-85937-061-6	£12.99
Bristol (pb)	1-85937-264-3	£9.99	Edinburgh (pb)	1-85937-193-0	£8.99
British Life A Century Ago (pb)	1-85937-213-9	£9.99	England in the 1880s	1-85937-331-3	£17.99
Buckinghamshire (pb)	1-85937-200-7	£9.99	English Castles (pb)	1-85937-434-4	£9.99
Camberley (pb)	1-85937-222-8	£9.99	English Country Houses	1-85937-161-2	£17.99
Cambridge (pb)	1-85937-422-0	£9.99	Essex (pb)	1-85937-270-8	£9.99
Cambridgeshire (pb)	1-85937-420-4	£9.99	Exeter	1-85937-126-4	£12.99
Canals & Waterways (pb)	1-85937-291-0	£9.99	Exmoor	1-85937-132-9	£14.99
Canterbury Cathedral (pb)	1-85937-179-5	£9.99	Falmouth	1-85937-066-7	£12.99
Cardiff (pb)	1-85937-093-4	£9.99	Folkestone (pb)	1-85937-124-8	£9.99
Carmarthenshire	1-85937-216-3	£14.99	Glasgow (pb)	1-85937-190-6	£9.99
Chelmsford (pb)	1-85937-310-0	£9.99	Gloucestershire	1-85937-102-7	£14.99
Cheltenham (pb)	1-85937-095-0	£9.99	Great Yarmouth (pb)	1-85937-426-3	£9.99
Cheshire (pb)	1-85937-271-6	£9.99	Greater Manchester (pb)	1-85937-266-x	£9.99
Chester	1-85937-090-x	£12.99	Guildford (pb)	1-85937-410-7	£9.99
Chesterfield	1-85937-378-x	£9.99	Hampshire (pb)	1-85937-279-1	£9.99
Chichester (pb)	1-85937-228-7	£9.99	Hampshire Churches (pb)	1-85937-207-4	£9.99
Colchester (pb)	1-85937-188-4	£8.99	Harrogate	1-85937-423-9	£9.99
Cornish Coast	1-85937-163-9	£14.99	Hastings & Bexhill (pb)	1-85937-131-0	£9.99
Cornwall (pb)	1-85937-229-5	£9.99	Heart of Lancashire (pb)	1-85937-197-3	£9.99
Cornwall Living Memories	1-85937-248-1	£14.99	Helston (pb)	1-85937-214-7	£9.99
Cotswolds (pb)	1-85937-230-9	£9.99	Hereford (pb)	1-85937-175-2	£9.99
Cotswolds Living Memories	1-85937-255-4	£14.99	Herefordshire	1-85937-174-4	£14.99
County Durham	1-85937-123-x	£14.99	Hertfordshire (pb)	1-85937-247-3	£9.99
Croydon Living Memories	1-85937-162-0	£9.99	Horsham (pb)	1-85937-432-8	£9.99
Cumbria	1-85937-101-9	£14.99	Humberside	1-85937-215-5	£14.99
Dartmoor	1-85937-145-0	£14.99	Hythe, Romney Marsh & Ashford	1-85937-256-2	£9.99

Available from your local bookshop or from the publisher

Frith Book Co Titles (continued)

Ipswich (pb)	1-85937-424-7	£9.99	St Ives (pb)	1-85937415-8	£9.99
Ireland (pb)	1-85937-181-7	£9.99	Scotland (pb)	1-85937-182-5	£9.99
Isle of Man (pb)	1-85937-268-6	£9.99	Scottish Castles (pb)	1-85937-323-2	£9.99
Isles of Scilly	1-85937-136-1	£14.99	Sevenoaks & Tunbridge	1-85937-057-8	£12.99
Isle of Wight (pb)	1-85937-429-8	£9.99	Sheffield, South Yorks (pb)	1-85937-267-8	£9.99
Isle of Wight Living Memories	1-85937-304-6	£14.99	Shrewsbury (pb)	1-85937-325-9	£9.99
Kent (pb)	1-85937-189-2	£9.99	Shropshire (pb)	1-85937-326-7	£9.99
Kent Living Memories	1-85937-125-6	£14.99	Somerset	1-85937-153-1	£14.99
Lake District (pb)	1-85937-275-9	£9.99	South Devon Coast	1-85937-107-8	£14.99
Lancaster, Morecambe & Heysham (pb)	1-85937-233-3	£9.99	South Devon Living Memories	1-85937-168-x	£14.99
Leeds (pb)	1-85937-202-3	£9.99	South Hams	1-85937-220-1	£14.99
Leicester	1-85937-073-x	£12.99	Southampton (pb)	1-85937-427-1	£9.99
Leicestershire (pb)	1-85937-185-x	£9.99	Southport (pb)	1-85937-425-5	£9.99
Lincolnshire (pb)	1-85937-433-6	£9.99	Staffordshire	1-85937-047-0	£12.99
Liverpool & Merseyside (pb)	1-85937-234-1	£9.99	Stratford upon Avon	1-85937-098-5	£12.99
London (pb)	1-85937-183-3	£9.99	Suffolk (pb)	1-85937-221-x	£9.99
Ludlow (pb)	1-85937-176-0	£9.99	Suffolk Coast	1-85937-259-7	£14.99
Luton (pb)	1-85937-235-x	£9.99	Surrey (pb)	1-85937-240-6	£9.99
Maidstone	1-85937-056-x	£14.99	Sussex (pb)	1-85937-184-1	£9.99
Manchester (pb)	1-85937-198-1	£9.99	Swansea (pb)	1-85937-167-1	£9.99
Middlesex	1-85937-158-2	£14.99	Tees Valley & Cleveland	1-85937-211-2	£14.99
New Forest	1-85937-128-0	£14.99	Thanet (pb)	1-85937-116-7	£9.99
Newark (pb)	1-85937-366-6	£9.99	Tiverton (pb)	1-85937-178-7	£9.99
Newport, Wales (pb)	1-85937-258-9	£9.99	Torbay	1-85937-063-2	£12.99
Newquay (pb)	1-85937-421-2	£9.99	Truro	1-85937-147-7	£12.99
Norfolk (pb)	1-85937-195-7	£9.99	Victorian and Edwardian Cornwall	1-85937-252-x	£14.99
Norfolk Living Memories	1-85937-217-1	£14.99	Victorian & Edwardian Devon	1-85937-253-8	£14.99
Northamptonshire	1-85937-150-7	£14.99	Victorian & Edwardian Kent	1-85937-149-3	£14.99
Northumberland Tyne & Wear (pb)	1-85937-281-3	£9.99	Vic & Ed Maritime Album	1-85937-144-2	£17.99
North Devon Coast	1-85937-146-9	£14.99	Victorian and Edwardian Sussex	1-85937-157-4	£14.99
North Devon Living Memories	1-85937-261-9	£14.99	Victorian & Edwardian Yorkshire	1-85937-154-x	£14.99
North London	1-85937-206-6	£14.99	Victorian Seaside	1-85937-159-0	£17.99
North Wales (pb)	1-85937-298-8	£9.99	Villages of Devon (pb)	1-85937-293-7	£9.99
North Yorkshire (pb)	1-85937-236-8	£9.99	Villages of Kent (pb)	1-85937-294-5	£9.99
Norwich (pb)	1-85937-194-9	£8.99	Villages of Sussex (pb)	1-85937-295-3	£9.99
Nottingham (pb)	1-85937-324-0	£9.99	Warwickshire (pb)	1-85937-203-1	£9.99
Nottinghamshire (pb)	1-85937-187-6	£9.99	Welsh Castles (pb)	1-85937-322-4	£9.99
Oxford (pb)	1-85937-411-5	£9.99	West Midlands (pb)	1-85937-289-9	£9.99
Oxfordshire (pb)	1-85937-430-1	£9.99	West Sussex	1-85937-148-5	£14.99
Peak District (pb)	1-85937-280-5	£9.99	West Yorkshire (pb)	1-85937-201-5	£9.99
Penzance	1-85937-069-1	£12.99	Weymouth (pb)	1-85937-209-0	£9.99
Peterborough (pb)	1-85937-219-8	£9.99	Wiltshire (pb)	1-85937-277-5	£9.99
Piers	1-85937-237-6	£17.99	Wiltshire Churches (pb)	1-85937-171-x	£9.99
Plymouth	1-85937-119-1	£12.99	Wiltshire Living Memories	1-85937-245-7	£14.99
Poole & Sandbanks (pb)	1-85937-251-1	£9.99	Winchester (pb)	1-85937-428-x	£9.99
Preston (pb)	1-85937-212-0	£9.99	Windmills & Watermills	1-85937-242-2	£17.99
Reading (pb)	1-85937-238-4	£9.99	Worcester (pb)	1-85937-165-5	£9.99
Romford (pb)	1-85937-319-4	£9.99	Worcestershire	1-85937-152-3	£14.99
Salisbury (pb)	1-85937-239-2	£9.99	York (pb)	1-85937-199-x	£9.99
Scarborough (pb)	1-85937-379-8	£9.99	Yorkshire (pb)	1-85937-186-8	£9.99
St Albans (pb)	1-85937-341-0	£9.99	Yorkshire Living Memories	1-85937-166-3	£14.99

See Frith books on the internet www.francisfrith.co.uk

FRITH PRODUCTS & SERVICES

Francis Frith would doubtless be pleased to know that the pioneering publishing venture he started in 1860 still continues today. A hundred and forty years later, The Francis Frith Collection continues in the same innovative tradition and is now one of the foremost publishers of vintage photographs in the world. Some of the current activities include:

Interior Decoration

Today Frith's photographs can be seen framed and as giant wall murals in thousands of pubs, restaurants, hotels, banks, retail stores and other public buildings throughout the country. In every case they enhance the unique local atmosphere of the places they depict and provide reminders of gentler days in an increasingly busy and frenetic world.

Product Promotions

Frith products are used by many major companies to promote the sales of their own products or to reinforce their own history and heritage. Frith promotions have been used by Hovis bread, Courage beers, Scots Porage Oats, Colman's mustard, Cadbury's foods, Mellow Birds coffee, Dunhill pipe tobacco, Guinness, and Bulmer's Cider.

Genealogy and Family History

As the interest in family history and roots grows world-wide, more and more people are turning to Frith's photographs of Great Britain for images of the towns, villages and streets where their ancestors lived; and, of course, photographs of the churches and chapels where their ancestors were christened, married and buried are an essential part of every genealogy tree and family album.

Frith Products

All Frith photographs are available Framed or just as Mounted Prints and Posters (size 23 x 16 inches). These may be ordered from the address below. From time to time other products - Address Books, Calendars, Table Mats, etc - are available.

The Internet

Already twenty thousand Frith photographs can be viewed and purchased on the internet through the Frith websites and a myriad of partner sites.

For more detailed information on Frith companies and products, look at these sites:

www.francisfrith.co.uk
www.francisfrith.com
(for North American visitors)

See the complete list of Frith Books at:

www.francisfrith.co.uk

This web site is regularly updated with the latest list of publications from the Frith Book Company. If you wish to buy books relating to another part of the country that your local bookshop does not stock, you may purchase on-line.

For further information, trade, or author enquiries please contact us at the address below:
The Francis Frith Collection, Frith's Barn, Teffont, Salisbury, Wiltshire, England SP3 5QP.
Tel: +44 (0)1722 716 376 Fax: +44 (0)1722 716 881   Email: sales@francisfrith.co.uk

See Frith books on the internet www.francisfrith.co.uk

TO RECEIVE YOUR FREE MOUNTED PRINT

Mounted Print
Overall size 14 x 11 inches

Cut out this Voucher and return it with your remittance for £2.25 to cover postage and handling, to UK addresses. For overseas addresses please include £4.00 post and handling. Choose any photograph included in this book. Your SEPIA print will be A4 in size, and mounted in a cream mount with burgundy rule line, overall size 14 x 11 inches.

Order additional Mounted Prints at HALF PRICE (only £7.49 each*)

If there are further pictures you would like to order, possibly as gifts for friends and family, purchase them at half price (no additional postage and handling required).

Have your Mounted Prints framed*

For an additional £14.95 per print you can have your chosen Mounted Print framed in an elegant polished wood and gilt moulding, overall size 16 x 13 inches (no additional postage and handling required).

---

* IMPORTANT!
These special prices are only available if ordered using the original voucher on this page (no copies permitted) and at the same time as your free Mounted Print, for delivery to the same address

---

Frith Collectors' Guild

From time to time we publish a magazine of news and stories about Frith photographs and further special offers of Frith products. If you would like 12 months FREE membership, please return this form.

Send completed forms to:
The Francis Frith Collection, Frith's Barn, Teffont, Salisbury, Wiltshire SP3 5QP

Voucher for FREE and Reduced Price Frith Prints

Picture no.	Page number	Qty	Mounted @ £7.49	Framed + £14.95	Total Cost
		1	**Free of charge***	£	£
			£7.49	£	£
			£7.49	£	£
			£7.49	£	£
			£7.49	£	£
			£7.49	£	£

Please allow 28 days for delivery	*** Post & handling**	£2.25
Book Title	**Total Order Cost**	£

Please do not photocopy this voucher. Only the original is valid, so please cut it out and return it to us.

I enclose a cheque / postal order for £ . . . . made payable to 'The Francis Frith Collection' OR please debit my Mastercard / Visa / Switch / Amex card *(credit cards please on all overseas orders)*

Number . . . .

Issue No(Switch only) . . . . .Valid from (Amex/Switch) . . . .

Expires . . . . Signature . . . .

Name Mr/Mrs/Ms . . . .

Address . . . .

. . . .

. . . .

Postcode . . . . Daytime Tel No . . . .

Email Address . . . .

Valid to 31/12/04

The Francis Frith Collectors' Guild

Please enrol me as a member for 12 months free of charge.

Name Mr/Mrs/Ms . . . .

Address . . . .

. . . .

. . . .

. . . . Postcode . . . .

Would you like to find out more about Francis Frith?

We have recently recruited some entertaining speakers who are happy to visit local groups, clubs and societies to give an illustrated talk documenting Frith's travels and photographs. If you are a member of such a group and are interested in hosting a presentation, we would love to hear from you.

Our speakers bring with them a small selection of our local town and county books, together with sample prints. They are happy to take orders. A small proportion of the order value is donated to the group who have hosted the presentation. The talks are therefore an excellent way of fundraising for small groups and societies.

Can you help us with information about any of the Frith photographs in this book?

We are gradually compiling an historical record for each of the photographs in the Frith archive. It is always fascinating to find out the names of the people shown in the pictures, as well as insights into the shops, buildings and other features depicted.

If you recognize anyone in the photographs in this book, or if you have information not already included in the author's caption, do let us know. We would love to hear from you, and will try to publish it in future books or articles.

Our production team

Frith books are produced by a small dedicated team at offices in the converted Grade II listed 18th-century barn at Teffont near Salisbury, illustrated above. Most have worked with the Frith Collection for many years. All have in common one quality: they have a passion for the Frith Collection. The team is constantly expanding, but currently includes:

Jason Buck, John Buck, Douglas Burns, Ruth Butler, Heather Crisp, Isobel Hall, Hazel Heaton, Peter Horne, James Kinnear, Tina Leary, Hannah Marsh, Sue Molloy, Kate Rotondetto, Dean Scource, Eliza Sackett, Terence Sackett, Sandra Sanger, Lewis Taylor, Shelley Tolcher, Clive Wathen and Jenny Wathen.